Williamsburg's Glorious Gardens

Williamsburg's

THE COLONIAL WILLIAMSBURG FOUNDATION
WILLIAMSBURG, VIRGINIA

Glorious Gardens

PHOTOGRAPHY BY ROGER FOLEY

Governor's Palace Garden (*right*):
Common boxwood topiary (*Buxus sempervirens*);
Common foxglove (*Digitalis purpurea*);
Sweet William (*Dianthus barbatus*); English daisy (*Bellis perennis*)

Chiswell-Bucktrout Garden (*overleaf*):
Mixed colors lily-flowered tulip (*Tulipa Gesnerana*)

Text ©1996 by The Colonial Williamsburg Foundation
Photographs ©1996 by Roger Foley
Second printing, 1997

Library of Congress Cataloging-in-Publication Data

Foley, Roger.
Williamsburg's Glorious Gardens / Photography by Roger Foley.
    p.   cm.
    ISBN 0-87935-160-8
    1. Gardens—Virginia—Williamsburg. 2. Gardens—Virginia
—Williamsburg—Pictorial Works. I. Colonial Williamsburg
Foundation. II. Title.
SB466.U65W55 1996
712'.09755'4252—dc20   95-40938
                                                        CIP

TEXT BY DONNA C. SHEPPARD
BOOK DESIGN BY JOEL AVIROM

Printed in Canada

Williamsburg's gardens change dramatically from season to season, from the serene green gardens of summer, the changing hues of fall, and the quiet structure of winter to the colorful excitement of spring. Gardens display a freshness in the spring that delights the senses and fills the gardener with anticipation. As gardeners we forget the drudgery of August's dog days, the annual drought, or the devastation from pestilence and pest. For the most dedicated gardener or one with a decidedly brown thumb, spring gardens are a delight.

Roger Foley's spring photography of Williamsburg's gardens captures the excitement of this annual rejuvenation. Roger spent countless days exploring the gardens, finding just the right angle from which to photograph a flower or just the proper moment during which to capture the image of a tiny garden in the fading light.

Roger's images of Williamsburg's gardens are virtually dominated by flowers. It has been said and often written that gardening is a labor of love. If this be true, then flowers are a gardener's greatest form of expression. These are the flowers of a bygone era, come to these shores from the British Isles, the European continent, some even from the Orient. Others are native American wildflowers brought into

the garden. All of these flowers were well known to the Virginia colonists.

Gardens are a perishable art form, and while the gardens of eighteenth-century Williamsburg did not survive to the twentieth century, today's gardens are the result of exhaustive research and design efforts and careful attention to every detail of their re-creation. The meticulous care of generations of skilled gardeners has provided countless visitors with the pleasures seen in these views of the gardens of Colonial Williamsburg.

GORDON W. CHAPPELL
DIRECTOR, LANDSCAPE AND FACILITIES SERVICES

SPRING BEGINS

The gardens in the Historic Area are one of the great joys of Colonial Williamsburg. In all seasons, in all weathers, Williamsburg's gardens make the city a sanctuary, a journey back to the time when the image of a "green country town" was an eighteenth-century ideal.

Blossom by blossom, spring begins. Walking through the gardens of Colonial Williamsburg's Historic Area on a balmy day is a reminder that spring holds the promise of eternal renewal. The redbuds with their distinctive purplish red flowers are the first to bloom. Then fruit trees—apples, peaches, pears, and plums—burst into flower. Their profuse blossoms emerge in white and in many shades of pink, and their delicate scents perfume the air. Next come the showy dogwoods, whose pure white blossoms spangle the wooded areas or serve as focal points in the re-created gardens.

Shy crocuses are followed by narcissi, blue and white hyacinths, anemones, and other flowering bulbs. Golden jonquils border walks, cluster on a hillside, meander along the banks of a stream.

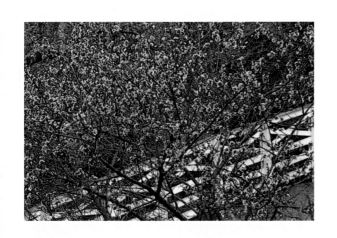

Visitors from far and near come to revel in the spectacular show of brilliant tulips—red in the Governor's Palace gardens, white in the oval planting bed at the Orlando Jones House, lily-flowered and Rembrandts in gardens throughout the Historic Area.

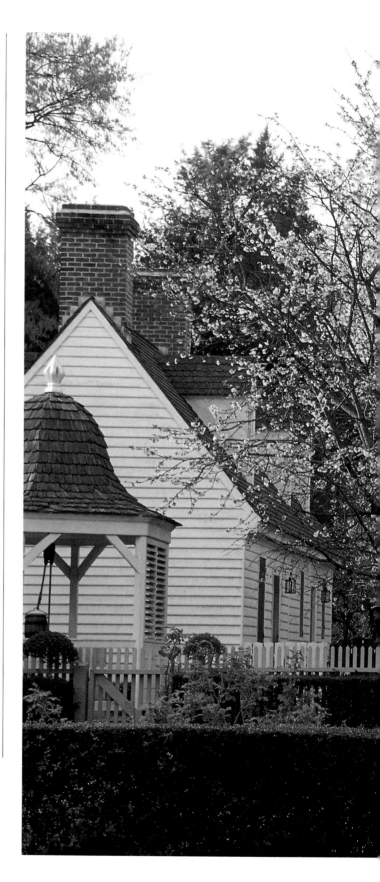

*A flowering crab apple
flourishes by the
George Pitt House.*

*Masses of white-flowering
crab apples, known locally as
the Chiswell crab apple, in
the Custis Tenement orchard.*

*Over time, dainty spring
starflowers have naturalized
everywhere in
the Historic Area.*

APRIL GLORY

As the chill of March gives way to April's warmth, spring comes with a rush in the gardens of Colonial Williamsburg. In early April, the white blossoms of flowering dogwoods, the state tree of Virginia, begin to unfurl. Fragrant lavender lilacs and showy red buckeyes add to the April glory.

The once tiny buds of spring-flowering bulbs open into exquisite flowers overnight. Soon the gardens contain a multitude of dainty jonquils, narcissi, grape hyacinths, and anemones. The profusion of gay tulips in an infinite variety of species and hues has become synonymous with spring in Williamsburg.

In colors as fresh as spingtime itself, the periwinkles, columbines, Johnny-jump-ups, bluebells, cowslips, and forget-me-nots that crowd the beds and borders vie for attention. From the formal, patterned plantings at the Governor's Palace to the secluded little flower-filled wilderness plot on Francis Street beside the Dr. Barraud House, the gardens of Colonial Williamsburg are filled with April's glory.

"I have a pretty little garden in which I take more satisfaction than in anything in this world," wrote John Custis, father of Martha Washington's first husband, to a friend in London in 1725. Visitors to Colonial Williamsburg's gardens in April would agree.

LEFT

A pleasing planting scheme along the fence in the Elkanah Deane garden includes coral columbines, purple and yellow Johnny-jump-ups, pink English daisies, lavender ajuga and ageratum, yellow English wallflowers, and brilliant golden yellow tulips.

*The border in the Taliaferro-Cole
garden features a diversity of plants:
assorted multi-color tulips, spring
starflowers, forget-me-nots, English
daisies, and Johnny-jump-ups.*

*Anemones in brilliant colors of
crimson, purple, fuchsia, and pink
grow at the east end of the garden.*

Delicately scented lilacs next to the Lightfoot House smokehouse; lily-flowered and Rembrandt tulips and anemones along the picket fence.

RIGHT

Crimson Renown tulips by the Lightfoot Tenement.

LEFT

Blue and white hyacinths and pink English daisies are at their peak in the Prentis garden. Tulips interplanted in the beds are just beginning to open.

RIGHT

Striped Keizerskroon tulips at the Governor's Palace.

ABOVE

*The squares at each end of the
formal pleasure garden at the
Prentis House are edged in
yaupon hollies and accented
with red buckeye trees
underplanted with spring bulbs.*

RIGHT

*Tulips in their infinite variety
are synonymous with
Williamsburg in the spring.*

LEFT
*Apple trees and buttercups
in the Deane orchard.*

ABOVE
*Daylilies encircle the base of
a white-flowering dogwood.
The beds closer to the Blue
Bell Tavern contain tulips
and English wallflowers.*

33

LEFT AND OPPOSITE RIGHT
Angelique tulips at the Governor's Palace.
CENTER
*Lilacs, Cherokee roses, and tree peonies
in the Bryan garden.*

LEFT
Forget-me-nots.
BELOW
Wood hyacinths.

Wisteria with its showy racemes of soft lavender flowers accents the rail fence at the site of Robertson's windmill.

LEFT

At the Governor's Palace, the interlaced branches
of American beeches form a shady allée.

ABOVE

The creamy white blossoms of a black haw contrast
with a pink-flowering dogwood.

BELOW

A pink-flowering horse chestnut.

English wallflowers and assorted tulips in the foreground with the Benjamin Powell House in the background.

62

The Cherokee rose has been
popular in southern gardens
since colonial days.
Governor Milledge of
Georgia sent some seeds to
Jefferson, who recorded in
his diary that he planted
them in his nursery garden.

MAY SPLENDOR

When May ushers in longer, warmer days, the plant materials in the Historic Area change yet again. Showy blooms appear on the stately catalpa trees that line Palace green, replacements for the ones growing there when Thomas Jefferson resided in Virginia's colonial capital. The golden-rain tree, which originally came from the Orient, displays handsome compound leaves and panicles of yellow flowers.

May belongs to the majestic iris, named for the Greek goddess of the rainbow. Colonial Virginians knew this stately flower, one of the oldest in cultivation, as "flag." Iris creates a beautiful color contrast in plantings with orange-red poppies and pink and white dianthus.

Shasta daisies, phlox, peonies, and larkspurs fill the gardens with the splendor of May. Gay foxgloves were grown in colonial Virginia for their bright colors and medicinal properties; foxgloves are a natural source of digitalis. May is also the season for daylilies. Their name—"Hemerocallis"—is from the Greek "hemera" and "kallow," meaning "day" and "beautiful," because each flower lasts but a single day, fading by nightfall.

Those who visit Colonial Williamsburg's gardens in the spring take inspiration from avid  gardener Thomas Jefferson, who wrote nearly two centuries ago: "No occupation is so delightful to me as the culture of the earth, and no culture comparable to that of the garden . . . though an old man, I am but a young gardener."

Foxgloves, English and Shasta daisies, poppies, iris, and dianthus grow in profusion in the Governor's Palace gardens.

LEFT

Ivy twines around the gnarled paper mulberry in the garden at the Taliaferro-Cole House.

ABOVE

Iris, feverfew, columbine, and spiderwort.

RIGHT

Shy Johnny-jump-ups.

Foxgloves were cultivated in colonial gardens for their showy tubular flowers and medicinal qualities.

LEFT

Mountain laurel at the Governor's Palace.

BELOW

Garden peas near the George Wythe office.

LEFT AND BELOW

*The Cherokee rose was cultivated by Williamsburg
gardeners in the eighteenth century.*

ABOVE

*A shadbush grows in the Alexander Purdie garden.
Colonial Virginians sometimes called this small tree
"Juneberry," "serviceberry," or "shadblow."*

Native to England and Europe, larkspur, an annual plant, was well known in early American gardens.

Spring holds the promise of eternal renewal.

Plant Materials Featured in Williamsburg's Glorious Gardens

1 Prentis Garden:
Common apple (*Malus pumila*)

3 Common plum (*Prunus domestica*)

4 Poet's narcissus (*Narcissus poeticus*)

5 Elizabeth Carlos Garden: Yaupon holly hedge (*Ilex vomitoria*); Sour cherry (*Prunus Cerasus* 'Montmorency')

6 George Pitt Garden (*left*): Wild sweet crab apple (*Malus coronaria*); Custis Tenement Garden (*right*): Wild sweet crab apple (*Malus coronaria*)

7 Spring starflower (*Ipheion uniflorum*)

8–9 Custis Tenement Garden: Wild sweet crab apple (*Malus coronaria*)

10–11 Poet's narcissus (*Narcissus poeticus*)

12–13 Prentis Garden: Single early tulip (*Tulipa Gesnerana*)

14–15 Taliaferro-Cole Garden

17 Single early tulip (*Tulipa Gesnerana*); Golden tulip (*Tulipa chrysantha*)

18 Elkanah Deane Garden: Single early tulip (*Tulipa Gesnerana*); Wild columbine (*Aquilegia canadensis*); English wallflower (*Cheiranthus Cheiri*); English daisy (*Bellis perennis*); Johnny-jump-up (*Viola tricolor*); Carpet bugleweed (*Ajuga reptans*)

19 Flowering dogwood (*Cornus florida*) (*above*) Common apple (*Malus pumila*) (*below*)

20–21 Yellow single early tulip (*Tulipa Gesnerana*); Johnny-jump-up (*Viola tricolor*)

22 Single early tulip (*Tulipa Gesnerana*); English daisy (*Bellis perennis*); Spring starflower (*Ipheion uniflorum*); Edging candytuft (*Iberis sempervirens*)

23 Windflower, anemone (*Anemone coronaria*)

24 Chiswell-Bucktrout Garden: Mixed colors tulip (*Tulipa Gesnerana*); Windflower, anemone (*Anemone coronaria*); Common lilac (*Syringa vulgarus*)

25 Lightfoot Tenement Garden: Common boxwood (*Buxus sempervirens*); Lily-flowered tulip (*Tulipa Gesnerana*); Single late tulip (*Tulipa Gesnerana*); Common lilac (*Syringa vulgaris*)

26 Prentis Garden: Hyacinth (*Hyacinthus orientalis*); English daisy (*Bellis perennis*)

27 English daisy (*Bellis perennis*) (*left*) Governor's Palace Garden (*right*): Keizerkroon tulip (*Tulipa Gesnerana*)

28 Prentis Garden: Mixed colors single tulip (*Tulipa Gesnerana*)

29 Tulip (mixed varieties) (*Tulipa Gesnerana*)

30–31 Lightfoot Tenement Garden: Red single late tulip (*Tulipa Gesnerana*)

32 Elkanah Deane Orchard: Common apple (*Malus pumila*); wild buttercup (*Ranunculus* sp.)

33 Blue Bell Tavern Garden: Flowering dogwood (*Cornus florida*); Single late tulip (*Tulipa Gesnerana*); English wallflower (*Cheiranthus Cheiri*); Tawny daylily (*Hemerocallis fulva*)

34 Governor's Palace Garden (*above left*): Common boxwood topiary (*Buxus sempervirens*); Christiana Campbell's Tavern Garden (*above right*): Yaupon holly topiary (*Ilex vomitoria*); Elkanah Deane Garden (*below left*): Common boxwood topiary (*Buxus sempervirens*); Bryan Garden (*below right*): Common boxwood topiary (*Buxus sempervirens*)

35 Blue Bell Tavern Garden: English wallflower (*Cheiranthus Cheiri*); Mixed colors single late tulip (*Tulipa Gesnerana*)

36 Moody Garden (*above*): Common boxwood hedge (*Buxus sempervirens*); Red lily-flowered tulip (*Tulipa Gesnerana*); Custis Tenement Garden (*below*): Red and white single tulip (*Tulipa Gesnerana*)

37 Wild columbine (*Aquilegia canadensis*); Mixed colors tulip (*Tulipa Gesnerana*)

38–39 Market Square Tavern Garden: Mixed colors single tulip (*Tulipa Gesnerana*) (*above*); Lily-flowered tulip (*Tulipa Gesnerana*) (*below*)

40–41 Chiswell-Bucktrout Garden: Mixed colors lily-flowered tulip (*Tulipa Gesnerana*); Windflower, anemone (*Anemone coronaria*); Yaupon holly topiary (*Ilex vomitoria*)

42 Red tulip (*Tulipa Gesnerana*)

43 Governor's Palace Garden: Red tulip (*Tulipa Gesnerana*); Common boxwood topiary (*Buxus sempervirens*); Yaupon holly topiary (*Ilex vomitoria*); American beech (*Fagus grandifolia*)

44–45 Governor's Palace Garden: Red tulip (*Tulipa Gesnerana*); English daisy (*Bellis perennis*); Wild columbine (*Aquilegia canadensis*); Oxeye daisy (*Chrysanthemum Leucanthemum*); Common boxwood topiary (*Buxus sempervirens*); Common boxwood hedge (*Buxus sempervirens*); American beech (*Fagus grandifolia*); White oak (*Quercus alba*)

46 Tulip (*Tulipa Gesnerana*) (*left*); Bryan Garden (*right*): Tree peony (*Paeonia suffruticosa*); Cherokee rose (*Rosa laevigata*)

47 Pink tulip (*Tulipa Gesnerana*)

48–49 Common lilac (*Syringa vulgaris*) (*left*); Wythe Garden (*center*): Common boxwood hedge (*Buxus sempervirens*); English bluebell (*Endymion non-scriptus*); Johnny-jump-up (*Viola tricolor*); English bluebell (*Endymion non-scriptus*) (*right*)

50 Garden forget-me-not (*Myosotis sylvatica*)

51 Governor's Palace Garden: English bluebell (*Endymion non-scriptus*)

52–53 Redbud (*Cercis*) (*left*); Chinese wisteria (*Wisteria sinensis*) (*right*)

54–55 Spanish bluebell (*Endymion hispanicus*); Windflower, anemone (*Anemone coronaria*) (*left*); Flag iris (*Iris X germanica*) (*center*); Alexander Purdie Garden (*right*): Yaupon holly topiary (*Ilex vomitoria*)

56–57 Oxeye daisy (*Chrysanthemum Leucanthemum*)

58–59 Governor's Palace Garden (*left*): Pleached American beech arbor (*Fagus grandifolia*); Black haw (*Viburnum prunifolium*) (*above right*); Dr. Barraud Garden (*below right*): Pink-flowering horse chestnut (*Aesculus X plantierensis*)

60 Pink-flowering horse chestnut (*Aesculus X plantierensis*)

61 Coral honeysuckle (*Lonicera sempervirens*)

62–63 Blue Bell Tavern Garden: Single late tulip (*Tulipa Gesnerana*); English wallflower (*Cheiranthus Cheiri*)

64–65 White double-flowering rose (*Rosa Fortuniana*); Cherokee rose (*Rosa laevigata*) (*inset*)

66–67 Cherokee rose (*Rosa laevigata*)

68–69 John Blair Herb Garden: Pot marigold (*Calendula officinalis*); Dame's rocket (*Hesperis matronalis*); Common foxglove (*Digitalis purpurea*); Edging candytuft (*Iberis sempervirens*); Rosa Mundi rose (*Rosa gallica 'Versicolor'*); Red valerian (*Centranthus ruber*); Chive (*Allium Schoenoprasum*); Common thyme (*Thymus vulgaris*)

71 Common foxglove (*Digitalis purpurea*)

72–73 Governor's Palace Garden: Tulip (*Tulipa Gesnerana*); Oxeye daisy (*Chrysanthemum Leucanthemum*) (*left*); Oxeye daisy (*Chrysanthemum Leucanthemum*); Tulip (*Tulipa Gesnerana*); English daisy (*Bellis perennis*); Flag iris (*Iris X germanica*) (*right*)

74 Flag iris (*Iris X germanica*)

75 Taliaferro-Cole Garden: Flag iris (*Iris X germanica*); Oriental poppy (*Papaver orientale*) (*top*); Sweet William (*Dianthus barbatus*); Oriental poppy (*Papaver orientale*); American wisteria (*Wisteria frutescens*) (*below*)

76–77 Governor's Palace Garden: English daisy (*Bellis perennis*); Grass pink (*Dianthus plumarius var. 'spotii'*); Sweet William (*Dianthus barbatus*); Oxeye daisy (*Chrysanthemum Leucanthemum*); Common foxglove (*Digitalis purpurea*); Flag iris (*Iris X germanica*)

78–79 Governor's Palace Garden: Common foxglove (*Digitalis purpurea*); Oxeye daisy (*Chrysanthemum Leucanthemum*); Oriental poppy (*Papaver orientale*)

80–81 George Wythe Garden: American wisteria (*Wisteria frutescens*)

82 English ivy (*Hedera Helix*); Paper mulberry (*Broussonetia papyrifera*)

83 Dutch iris (*Iris Xiphium var. praecox x Iris tingitana*) (*left*); Johnny-jump-up (*Viola tricolor*) (*right*)

84–85 Governor's Palace Garden: Cross vine (*Bignonia capreolata*)

86–87 John Blair Herb Garden: Common foxglove (*Digitalis purpurea*)

88–89 Common foxglove (*Digitalis purpurea*); Dame's rocket (*Hesperis matronalis*)

90–91 Governor's Palace Garden: Mountain laurel (*Kalmia latifolia*); George Wythe Vegetable Garden: Garden pea (*Pisum sativum*)

92–93 Taliaferro-Cole Garden: Rocket larkspur (*Consolida ambigua*) (*above left*); Rocket larkspur (*Consolida ambigua*) (*below left*); Rocket larkspur (*Consolida ambigua*); Oriental poppy (*Papaver orientale*) (*center*); Rocket larkspur (*Consolida ambigua*) (*above right*); Purple Fleabane (*Erigeron sp.*) (*below right*)

94–95 Sweet William (*Dianthus barbatus*)

96 Brush-Everard Garden: Rosa 'Dorothy Perkins'

97 Rosa 'Shailer's Provence'

98–99 Rosa 'Dorothy Perkins'

100–101 Apothecary rose (*Rosa gallica 'Officinalis'*)

102 Cherokee rose sport (*Rosa laevigata*)

103 Alexander Purdie Garden: Shadbush (*Amelanchier canadensis*) (*above*); Cherokee rose sport (*Rosa laevigata*) (*below*)

104–105 Alexander Purdie Garden: Smoke tree (*Cotinus Coggygria*)

106 Hall's Japanese honeysuckle (*Lonicera japonica 'Halliana'*); Common spiderwort (*Tradescantia virginiana*) (*above left*); Onion (*Allium Cepa*) (*above right*); Common rue (*Ruta graveolens*); Clove pink (*Dianthus caryophyllus*); Chive (*Allium Schoenoprasum*) (*below left*); Grass pink (*Dianthus plumarius*); Summer-sweet (*Clethra alnifolia*) (*below right*)

107 Governor's Palace Garden: Common foxglove (*Digitalis purpurea*)

108 Rocket larkspur (*Consolida ambigua*)

109 Taliaferro-Cole Garden: Rocket larkspur (*Consolida ambigua*)

110 Governor's Palace Garden: Espaliered common apple (*Malus pumila*); Beach plum (*Prunus maritima*); Tree boxwood (*Buxus sempervirens 'Arborescens'*); English ivy (*Hedera Helix*)

111 Cypress spurge (*Euphorbia Cyparissias*)

112–113 Palace Green: Western catalpa (*Catalpa speciosa*)

114–115 Oriental poppy (*Papaver orientale*); Sweet William (*Dianthus barbatus*); Rocket larkspur (*Consolida ambigua*)

116 American beech (*Fagus grandifolia*)

117 Tawny daylily (*Hemerocallis fulva*)